W9-AAF-355

# Chili
# Madness

# Chili Madness

## A Passionate Cookbook
## by Jane Butel

Photographs
by Jerry Darvin

**Workman Publishing
New York**

# Acknowledgments

Library of Congress Cataloging in Publication Data

Butel, Jane.
    Chili madness.
    Includes index.
    1. Chili con carne.  I. Title.
TX749.B87   641.8'2   80-51617
ISBN 0-89480-135-X
ISBN 0-89480-134-1 (pbk.)

Cover Illustration: Milton Glaser
Book Design: Florence Mayers
Photographs: Jerry Darvin

Workman Publishing Company, Inc.
1 West 39 Street
New York, New York 10018

Manufactured in the United States of America
First printing October 1980

10 9 8 7 6 5 4 3

I wish to acknowledge the always enthusiastic and capable assistance of Ann Weninger, Lark Wittens, Gwynne MacManus, Vivian Batts, my daughter Amy, and my mother. Also, Ben Roth and Santiago Moneo who were always ready to taste!

And, the many chili society buffs, particularly Jim West, Frank X. Tolbert, John Serotko and Jeanne Croft.

# Dedication

To my dad, who first taught me to like chili hot, and to Ben, who has helped me to understand those who don't.

# Contents

# The Irresistible Passion

# Origins of the Bowl of Blessedness

Whenever I meet someone who does not consider chili a favorite dish, then I've usually found someone who has never tasted good chili. No other food has inspired the passionate following that this dish has. I mean, I have yet to hear of a society dedicated to the appreciation of cheesecake, or a newspaper that deals solely with croissants, or renowned chefs quarreling over the ingredients for chocolate mousse.

Yet chili has all of these elements — dedicated societies, newspapers and quarrels, even a prayer — and much more. Something in the personality of this bowl of fire gave birth to an international cult movement. Chili lovers come from every walk of life. Chili attracts truck drivers, celebrities, doctors, lawyers, and schoolteachers. Rich and poor undergo a Jekyll/Hyde-like transformation and mild-mannered pillars of the community show no mercy when the topic of conversation turns to controversial chili.

America's favorite food is the subject of much controversy. It's all here including the creation of the dish, the spelling of its name, and the ingredients to include.

Their baptism by fire has made them missionaries for life.

While each chili lover has his/her own ingredients and methods, this band of passionate independents have come together in an organized network with rites and rituals and factions enough to rival a political machine. For many years their passions were kept under wraps. Although the first chili organization — the Chili Appreciation Society, International (CASI) — was founded in the 1950s and membership and attention grew consistently, especially in the Southwest, the rumble was merely portending the storm.

## Chili Fever
The tempest broke in 1966 when Frank X. Tolbert, chili lover, cook, and historian extraordinaire, published a book entitled, *A Bowl of Red*. Seeking to promote the book, Tolbert and his friends organized the first chili cookoff in Terlingua, Texas.

13

Untold numbers of chili lovers came out of the closet and traveled to this unearthly, forsaken patch of desert near the big bend of the Rio Grande river to witness the event. The main attraction was the pitting of Wick Fowler, chief cook of CASI, against

Long Photography
Courtesy of International Chili Society

H. Allen Smith. Originally Fowler's opponent was to have been Hollywood restaurateur and chili cook, Dave Chasen. But Chasen fell ill and a substitute had to be found. Smith, a New York-based writer and humorist, had written an article called "Nobody Knows More About Chili Than I Do," which was published in *Holiday* magazine in August 1967. Therein he lambasted Texas chili, totally riling every Texas chili cook. Smith was the perfect substitute for Chasen. And he could hardly turn down a challenge to his claim.

Sparked by this event, which ended in a tie, the infatuation with the bowl of red spilled over. The Chili Appreciation Society, International grew and rival organizations were formed. Today we see chili contests of every size held in all corners of the land—growing to be practically a national sport. Society newsletters carry news of activities; aficionados and novitiates travel hundreds of miles to be part of cookoffs and seminars. There's even a newspaper dedicated to "chiliheads and their ilk"—*The Goat Gap Gazette*.

**At the World's Championship Chili Cookoff held annually by the International Chili Society, the top chili chefs compete for first place, judged by a blue ribbon panel of food editors and celebrities.**

14

## The Great Chili Controversy

Chili cookoffs and debates are a result of years of feuds, spats, and heated rivalries — not to mention knock-down, drag-out fights. Who really makes the greatest chili?

New Mexicans are committed to the idea that chili must be pure — everything-but-the-kitchen-sink concoctions are unheard of, hissed and booed at and generally ignored. Traditionally, New Mexicans serve a saucy red chili puree or a green chili stew with sizable chunks of red meat with stewed pinto beans on the side. Heavy on the chile and light on the meat, New Mexican chili never contains any additional vegetables.

Next door in Texas (and elsewhere), however, chili nearly always contains coarse-ground beef, chile, garlic, cumin, and onions — and perhaps beans and tomatoes. Texans may even include such exotica as cinnamon or ground almonds.

Secrets abide, with some famous chili chefs swearing that their favorite recipes will die with them. Others, such as C. V. Wood, a founder of the International Chili Society, gladly share their techniques. Wood claims his secret is in the spices. He says "I always soak my spices in a can of beer. That natural carbonation releases flavors that don't come out any other way."

He advises simmering the spices and then cooling them in a refrigerator overnight before preparing the chili the next day. His chili was good enough to earn him the top prize in two world championships — 1969 and 1971.

---

**Chile or Chili?**

**Even the spelling of the name for a bowl of red is controversial. "Chili" as used in "chili con carne" is often spelled with an "i" ending. As far as I can determine, "chili" is an Eastern and Midwestern spelling that might be derived from the way the British spell it — "chilley." The other popular spelling, "chile," is based on the Mexican or Spanish spelling for the pod and is generally used to describe "chile" dishes in Mexican cooking. In this book, which is written for all serious chili lovers — "chiliheads" as they are known in the West — we are using the "chili" spelling for the dish, the "chile" spelling for the peppers, and "chili powder" for the commercial premixed blends.**

---

Carroll Shelby, another founder of the ICS, has a different view. He's very liberal about the basis of the brew, and says that chili is a matter of taste and inclination: "It's what you want when you make it. You can put in anything you feel like at the time. You make it one way one time, another time, a little different. Make it up to suit your mood."

Shelby's prowess surfaced way back in 1967 at the original cookoff where he whipped up batches of chili and just gave it away. It was so good, he developed a real going business out of selling his brown-paper-bagged chili fixings.

And, of course Frank S. Tolbert's book was so popular that he now satisfies thousands of chili lovers in Dallas at his own chili parlor. He advocates using only beef, onions, garlic, chile, and cumin.

So the controversy rages — you might say boils — on with questions of ingredients. Unresolved is the debate: whether or not to add beans — and if you do, should they be red, kidney, or pinto; there is the consistency question — thick versus thin. Should masa harina (corn flour) be added for additional substance. Should other meats — pork, chicken, duck, or wild game — accompany the ubiquitous beef. Lots of vegetables or almost none? Do out-of-the-ordinary ingredients — tequila, wine, raisins and whatnot — assist in building flavor? Who knows? One thing is certain — chili seems to only grow in popularity.

## The Legendary Origins

There is probably as much controversy surrounding the origin of the "bowl of blessedness," as Will Rogers called chili, as there is surrounding its ingredients. Only one thing seems to bear up under all scrutiny — chili did not originate in Mexico. While most of the stories about chili's genesis say that it is a product of gringos and tenderfeet, one rather fanciful tale as detailed in *Bull Cook and Authentic Historical Recipes and Practices* by George Herter, states that the first recipe for chili con carne was put on paper in the seventeenth century by a beautiful nun, Sister Mary of Agreda, mysteriously known to the Indians of the Southwest United States as the "lady in blue."

### Spiritual Beginnings

Legend has it that in 1618, at the age of sixteen, she entered a convent at Agreda in Castile, Spain. There, Sister Mary began to go into trances, with her body lifeless for days. When she awoke from these trances she said her spirit had been to a faraway land where she preached Christianity to savages and counseled them to seek out Spanish missionaries.

It is certain that Sister Mary never physically left Spain, yet Spanish missionaries and King Philip IV of Spain believed that she was the ghostly "La Dama de

Azul"—lady in blue—of Indian legend. For, there were many witnesses (including members of Indian tribes and a missionary, Father Alonso de Benarifes) of a holy woman who wore blue and worked among the Indians. When the Indians were shown a picture of Sister Mary they said that she was indeed their lady in blue, but that to them she was younger and more beautiful.

When Father Alonso returned to Spain he visited this nun with the visions. She vividly relayed to him scenes and people of the Southwest—things she could never have known unless she had been there, in some form.

Herter claims that Sister Mary wrote down the recipe for chili con carne on one of her "visits." It called for venison or antelope meat, onions, tomatoes, and chile peppers. But if Indians of the Southwest were indeed eating chili at the time of Sister Mary's "visit" during the Spanish occupation, no explorer recorded it—so who knows?

## Down to Earth Birth

Another notion, and one that seems based on fact rather than legend, is that the first chili mix was concocted around 1850 by Texan adventurers as a staple for hard times when traveling to and in the California gold fields. (Notice the Texas references, not Mexican, or even Nebraskan.) They supposedly pounded dried beef, fat, pepper, salt, and chile peppers together, all to be boiled later on the trail. E. DeGolyer, a knowledgeable chili scholar who first documented this version of the origin of chili, called it the "pemmican of the Southwest."

Maury Maverick, Jr. and Charles Ramsdell, two San Antonio writers, swear that chili con carne originated there, among the poor (this poor-peoples food is a continuing theme in many "origin-of-chili" tales). In an effort to stretch their

**A street scene in Falfurrias, Texas toward the end of the nineteenth century, around the time chili was first thought to have been created. It appears as if most of the locals were indoors downing bowls of their favorite brews when this photo was taken.**

The Heritage Museum, Falfurrias, Texas
Courtesy of Institute of Texan Cultures

slender budgets, they bought meat of poor quality, chopped it to the consistency of hash to make it tender, and added lots of chile pepper to give it flavor.

There are also some pretty tough customers who laid claim to the creation of chili — the residents of the Texas prisons in the mid to late 1800s. The Texas version of bread and water, or gruel — in other words, cheap prison fare — was a stew of the cheapest available ingredients: tough beef, hacked fine, chiles and spices, all boiled in water to an edible consistency. This "prisoner's plight" became a status symbol of the Texas prisons. Chain-gang chili is said to be among the best. Ex-cons who couldn't get a good bowl on the outside have allegedly broken parole so as to be recommitted — homesick for good chili! By the way, there's yet to be a story of an ex-con homesick for good gruel.

And lastly there is the very popular old standby: chili originated in Texas with the cowboys who were "winning the West." Needing hot, fill-up-the-stomach grub, the trail cooks came up with a sort of stew. Since chile peppers grew wild and there was plenty of beef around it was a logical, hearty and nutritious combination.

While there are many other stories

**Many think chili was born in the prisons of Texas as a way of making poor quality meat palatable. Prison cooks did such a good job that it has been said prisoners often hated being paroled knowing they would never find such tasty chili on the outside. This late nineteenth century woodcut shows prisoners marching in to dinner. Who knows, maybe it's chili.**

which are certainly entertaining, they seem to be more fancy than fact. Although chili by its nature is far more suited to this realm of tall tales than down-to-earth truths, I believe we must credit the Texas trail cooks who fed the cowboys as they "won the West" for originating the dish.

Certainly by the late 1800s chili had arrived, with San Antonio the chili center of the day. In the evening customers would stroll down to one of the city's plazas and partake of a bowl served up by one of the many outdoor vendors. In fact, it seems a night was not complete without a visit to one of these chili "queens," the women who served their brews from bubbling cauldrons behind gaudy booths. The smells permeated the air, inviting passers-by to taste.

The chili queens "spiced up" the night in San Antonio until 1943 when they were put out of business due to their inability to conform to sanitary standards enforced in the town's restaurants. Of course, by that time chili had already taken hold across Texas and the rest of the U.S. and was well on its way to becoming one of the country's best-loved dishes.

**You can be pretty sure that the Plaza Dining Rooms of El Paso, Texas, shown here circa 1900, included as one of its 25 cent, "strictly American" meals, a heaping bowl or two of fiery chili.**

**Many a good time was had and plenty of good chili was eaten at the chili stands run by the chili queens of San Antonio's west side.**

# Chili Makings

**Chipolte Chiles**

**Cascabel Chiles**

The pulsating, pleasurable, passion-producing pot of paradise known as chili has its beginnings with the chile pepper. Chiles are part of the pod-bearing capsicum family which encompasses five species and more than 300 plant varieties. They range from the peppers that produce the mild-mannered ground paprika to those fiery, eye-watering varieties that really make you sit up and take notice. Pure chile peppers which you grind fresh yourself, or those which are pre-ground and securely packaged give your "bowl of blessedness" the wonderful flavors that only come from the most careful preparation.

Chiles are very distinguishable from one another, although getting acquainted can be a bit mystifying at first. The first thing you need to know is that a chile pepper is eaten both in its unripe green and its ripe red stages. Just like fruit (which chiles really are), the green unripe chile has a tarter, "crisper" flavor than a mature red

What goes into a good bowl of chili? Chile peppers, the heart of the brew, are described, plus all the other spices and ingredients.

one. The ripening process converts the starch in the green chile to a sugar, producing a sweeter, more robust flavor.

## The Heart of Chili

Both red and green chiles of all kinds have unique roles in Mexican and Tex-Mex cooking. Fresh red chile peppers are available in the United States but only regionally and only in the late fall. In their dried whole, crushed or pure ground forms they are available year round and are the gemstone — the basis — for chili con carne.

So many people are unaware that chile peppers themselves have flavor, for all the chili powder they are likely to have experienced has only been hot and rank-tasting by virtue of blending the pure ground chile with oregano, cumin, salt, and garlic. These are the constituents of standard chili powder — sometimes with added masa or corn flour. Almost without exception, this mixture is sold in drastically inferior packaging that allows oxidation of the chile pepper. The flavor

### And Columbus Misnamed Them Peppers

Why are chiles which are technically members of the "capsicum" family, called "peppers"?

When the Spanish arrived in the Caribbean looking for a shorter water route to the East they sampled the unusual red pods the Indians used to spice up their food, and which gave the food a pungency that seemed to them similar to the valuable black pepper they knew. In the mistaken belief that they had found a new "family" member, the Spanish called the pod pepper. Now we know there is no botanical relationship between the pod and the peppercorn . . . although, the name has stuck.

evaporates leaving the powder with only the heat that has been captured in the oils. (All chiles have oil in their veins and seeds that work to retain the "heat.") Using this hot, usually stale powder is what ruins lots of chili. Good packaging is opaque and prevents oxidation of the spices.

It is also important to remember that when you use the commercial blends, the range of flavor possibilities is much

21

**California
Hybrid Chile**

narrower—you must accept the manufacturer's idea of how chili should taste, not yours. If you don't want to buy this mass appeal, blend your own, always using pure ground chiles and the freshest additional spices possible.

## Domestic Chiles

Besides ground chile, many chili and chili accompaniment recipes call for fresh or dried peppers in other forms. The most abundant, most popular, and most used chiles nationwide are the domestic hybrids developed in California and New Mexico and still largely grown there. They are broad shouldered, about two to three inches wide at the stem end and about five to seven inches long, on the average, with a pointed tip.

In selecting fresh green chiles, a rule of thumb is that the darker the color, the more pointed the tip and the narrower the shoulders, the hotter they will be. Similarly, the larger the pepper—particularly across the shoulders—the milder. This is generally true and is perhaps the most helpful guideline when picking and purchasing chiles. Since the peppers freely cross-pollinate, consistency in hotness is impossible even in peppers coming from the same plant. Just watch out for those tiny slope-shouldered little devils. Undiluted, they can produce pure pain in

22

even the most asbestos-mouthed.

In the Southwest—and increasingly throughout the rest of the country—chiles are sold fresh and green, particularly in the summer and fall months. They can be prepared and frozen for enjoyment later when fresh are no longer available (see page 26). In some areas of the country they are also available already chopped and frozen but the most widely available forms are the canned varieties: whole or diced green chiles.

## A Bowl A Day Keeps the Doctor Away

Devoted chiliheads have long felt that a rousing bowl of chili, served in good company, definitely increases a sense of well-being and general peace of mind. But, in addition to soothing the soul, it may also do good things for the body.

Erna Fergusson, author of *The Mexican Cookbook* feels a chile pepper "protects against colds and malaria, it aids digestion, it clarifies the blood, it develops robustness and resistance to the elements. It even acts as a stimulant to the romantically inclined."

A professor at the University of Pennsylvania, Dr. Paul Rozin, agrees that chile peppers aid digestion, adding they make heavier foods, such as tortillas and rice, easier to eat by causing salivation, gastric secretion, and gut movement.

Dr. Lora Shields, a biologist and native New Mexican, has a seriously founded "chile pepper theory." Noting the low incidence of heart disease among Spanish Americans and Indians of the Southwest, she studied these people to see if she could find out why. The common denominator, it seems, was their conspicuous use of chile peppers in so many of their dishes. Dr. Shields feels "the action of chile peppers consumed often and liberally may rid the body of enough fats to lower the consumers' blood-fat (cholesterol) level and reduce their chances of having a heart attack."

Others say that chili makes the heart beat faster, causing you to perspire. Sweat, you know, is your body's air conditioner—so maybe you should try eating chili on a hot summer day to cool you down.

**Anaheim Chile**

## Other Types of Chiles

Ancho chiles:

Sometimes called Mexican chiles — these are difficult to find outside Mexico or along the border, except in Mexican specialty stores. When green, they closely resemble the bell pepper in appearance, but have a much spicier flavor. Anchos are about three to four inches in diameter with waxy skins. They dry to a deep red, almost black color and are often blended with the domestic mild Anaheim variety in commercial chili powders.

Jalapeño chiles:

A popular additive for super-hot chili lovers. These small-to-medium-sized fiery monsters are dark green, about two and a half inches long, and about one inch in diameter, firm and round. They are generally available canned, pickled in olive oil, in most supermarkets. To use, the seeds, veins, and stems are removed and the flesh chopped into minuscule pieces for spicing up the pot.

**Jalapeño Chile**

**Pequin Chiles**

**Ancho Chile**

Pequin chiles:

A native chile that grows wild along the Mexican border and is popular with hotheads. Pequin is the most devilishly hot of all and is usually not easy to find although it is available in specialty stores in its dried form. It's really only recommended for those who have absolutely fireproof palates or a satanic addiction.

Serrano chiles:
Few people select this piping hot little pepper, popular in Mexico, for their chili recipes. It is difficult to find in the U.S., except in Mexican specialty stores. Tiny — skinny and only about one to one and a half inches long, it can make you cry or cough just by cutting one open! Rarely available fresh, it is generally pickled.

**Serrano Chiles**

While there are many, many other types of chile, they are rarely used in chili con carne. Some people use cayenne pepper or hot liquid pepper sauce in their recipes. To my way of thinking, they are acceptable alternate hot, hot sources, but not as authentic in flavor as those mentioned above.

## Preparing Chile Peppers:
Despite its strength, the flavor of the chile pepper is fragile and is present in the flesh of the chile pod. The ribs, seeds, and stems are the hottest parts and should be removed for the best flavor. The skins are

### Chiles: Too Hot To Handle

Before you get up to your elbows in fresh or dried whole chile peppers, let me warn you — handling those dynamos with your bare hands can have uncomfortable results!

Although some "wise sages" say that buttering your hands before you get started will prevent chile burn, I haven't found that this works. Wear rubber gloves, don't experiment with other preventives. And, never rub your hands against your eyes, nose or mouth. The tissue in these areas is extremely sensitive to the chile oils and fumes.

After working with chiles, wash both your hands and your rubber gloves thoroughly with soap and water.

If you're stubborn, as many a chilihead is, and you've ignored my warning, treat the burn as you would any other burn. Doctor it up with a paste of baking soda and water or a commercial burn ointment. If you have an aloe plant, break off a piece and rub the cut end against your sore fingers for natural relief.

tough and it is a good idea to remove them if you are using whole chiles. If fresh, parch to remove the skin.

To Parch Fresh Red or Green Chiles:
**1.** Rinse and drain the chiles. Pierce each chile once near the stem with the sharp point of a knife. If the chile is large, pierce a second time, near the tip.

**2.** Spread the chiles on an aluminum foil-covered cookie sheet and broil them rapidly until they brown and blister. Be sure to turn them as they blister.

**3.** As soon as they are evenly browned, remove the chiles from the cookie sheet and place them in a cold, damp towel (refrigerate the towel for half an hour) and allow them to steam. After approximately ten minutes, remove the chiles and peel for immediate use, or place in plastic bags, unpeeled, for use at a later date. (The peppers can be frozen at this point. Each bag should contain a dozen or so peppers, depending on the size of the bag and the size of the peppers, and should be sealed and labeled with the type of pepper and the date parched on the label. The skins will come off easily when thawed.) Peel them down in long strips.

**4.** Pull the stem off and, holding the chile point up, squeeze the pod from the point downward and the seeds will squirt out.

Some people like to pulverize whole chiles in a blender or food processor instead of parching and peeling. Personally, I'm not fond of this flavor, preferring them parched and peeled — or, better still, dried and ground or crushed for caribe-style flakes.

To Grind Dried Chiles:
Rinse, dry, and remove the seeds, stem, and veins of each dried pod. Place about four to six in an electric blender jar or food processor and blend until finely powdered. Repeat the process if more are needed.

Chile Caribe:
Rinse, dry, and remove the stems, then crush or tear the dried chiles with your hands into little pieces (approximately ¼-inch). Chile caribe can contain a portion of the seeds of the pepper. Red pepper flakes, sold in most supermarkets, have the look of chile caribe but they are usually the Italian type pepper and impart a different flavor.

Canned or Frozen Chiles:
To use the green chiles that come diced in cans or frozen, just add to taste. You need not defrost. If you buy the canned whole chiles, rinse them, pick out the stems and seeds, and use as desired.

## Other Essential Ingredients

As important as the spicy peppers are, there are other necessary ingredients for making good chili. These include appropriate seasonings such as cumin — usually ground — the fresher the better; fresh, pungent garlic and dried crushed or ground Mexican oregano. Mexican oregano is important to chili because its flavor is milder than the Greek or Italian varieties and so is less likely to overwhelm the flavor of the stew. It is available mainly by mail order or in specialty food stores (see page 90 for a listing).

Other than the spices, beef is the mainstay of chili. It should be prepared in either very fine cubes or be very coarsely chopped for the best flavor and consistency. This preparation is often referred to as "chili grind" (see page 32 for preparation instructions). Outside the Southwest, chili is generally made with hamburger-grind beef — only acceptable to real chili lovers if quality meat, not inedible trimmings, is used.

Besides the basics, many people like to improvise with other kinds of meat and of course, there are some very popular vegetables. For example, pork is used in a variety of chili recipes and makes a pleasant-tasting change. It should also be cubed, and sometimes can be blended with beef. And there are people — such as C.V. Woods, one of the stalwarts of the chili circuit — who cook up their favorite brew using chicken.

Onions of most any type help make excellent chili — some say the more you

---

**Chili-Combos**

The farther you get from Texas, the epicenter of chili's birthplace and the region of greatest dedication, the greater the variations.

■ All over the country chili, having really arrived, lends a zing to those familiar favorites the ubiquitous frankfurter (the chili-dog, of course) and the humble hamburger (the all-American chili-burger).

■ Cincinnatians sometimes add lettuce and invariably serve chili over a bed of spaghetti.

■ Louisvillians stir in broken tamales, usually the canned variety.

■ Kansas Citians go totally American and serve chili over macaroni, sometimes even baking them together in a casserole well known to school kids as chili-mac.

■ And admittedly variations pop up even in Texas. Dallasites have honored Fritos — a hometown product — with a concoction of chili over Fritos, cheese, and onions. They call it Frito pie.

---

27

cry when peeling and chopping, the better the chili. Seriously, though, white or yellow ordinary round onions are generally preferred. Sweet purple or Bermuda onions are generally not as flavorful although some recipes call for this type.

The addition of other vegetables, as well as onions, creates a lot of discussion. In defiance to traditionalists, some feel that tomatoes in one form or another are an absolute must. Other folks, myself included, disagree.

Beans are another controversial ingredient. New Mexicans feel stewed pinto beans should be served as a side dish, never blended into the stew. Texans are often partial to adding beans. If beans are added, the next question becomes what type—pinto, red, or kidney. My opinion, if any beans are used, is that pintos are the only true chili beans. They are authentically Western, the others are not. Californians will disagree, they and Midwesterners outspokenly prefer kidney beans. (Midwesterners have even used butter beans.) As a general guide: pinto beans have a meaty flavor; red or kidney beans are somewhat sweet tasting; you can decide for yourself about butter beans.

Definitely optional (yet increasingly used) vegetables are celery and bell pepper. Rarely seen (but often tossed in during a chili contest in order to create a flavor difference in hopes of stimulating a judge's palate) are raisins, almonds, barley, or alcoholic spirits such as beer, wine, or tequila.

Texture and consistency is another area of disagreement. Some prefer thin chili, others think thick. Masa—the cornmeal treated with lye for tamale or tortilla making, and available in Mexican specialty stores—is often used as a thickening. Some prefer to thicken the mixture by stewing it for a very long time and/or using very little liquid in the preparation. Generally, Easterners like it thicker than their Western cousins.

Given all the controversy surrounding this great American dish, and in the interests of good will and understanding, I dedicate this book to individualism. I have included recipes from chili contest winners and from other formidable chili chefs. Some recipes are made with beef, others with pork; some contain tomatoes, beans, celery, and spices traditionalists would question, and others are pure as can be. They are all tested and the cream of the chili crop. Try them all—they are delicious.

## Go Togethers

There's more in heaven than just chili. Any of these side dishes will complement its terrific flavor and dress up your table as well: Avocado and lime slices, raw celery and carrot sticks, chopped onions, finely chopped jalapeños, dill pickles, tostados, or soft tortillas. Sour cream with lime wedges or mixed with lime juice and sprinkled with fresh chopped coriander, and bowls of grated fresh Monterey Jack or Cheddar cheese are also great accompaniments. Or, you might want to try your hand at a creamy coleslaw, guacamole (made with ripe avocado and at least one jalapeño added to your favorite recipe if it isn't included already) or a refreshing corn bread.

Chili is delicious served over a bed of stewed pinto, kidney, or red beans. If your chili recipe doesn't include beans, have your favorites on hand.

# Basic Training— Methods to Chili Madness

Chili-making, like jogging, is an individual, character-building sport. First you master a few basics and go through a short training period. Then you're ready to develop your own style and set your own limits.

In my years of making and sharing chili recipes and judging chili contests, I've witnessed many successes and failures 'twixt the pod and the pot. All of this experience has contributed to the development of what I call my Chili Fitness Plan, an approach which assures that, no matter how individualistic you become, your chili will stand a good chance of being of Olympic quality.

### Chili Fitness Plan
**1.** Begin by finding a big, ol' pot . . . maybe a kettle like the witches in *Macbeth* use. If you can't get one of those, Dutch ovens and bean pots are good because they have a generous open surface for simmering and a heavy bottom for smooth, even cooking.

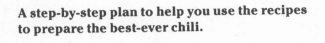

**A step-by-step plan to help you use the recipes to prepare the best-ever chili.**

Leave the lid to your pot in the cupboard. Never cover your chili while cooking — it inhibits flavor and texture development. Be sure to check your brew regularly. Leaving the lid off allows the liquid to evaporate more quickly and you will probably need to add more during the simmering stage. You will also need to stir occasionally to prevent sticking and insure even cooking.

**2.** Your chili deserves the best ingredients you can muster. As I've said before, pure ground chile pepper blended with fresh garlic, dried Mexican oregano, and dried ground (or whole) cumin seed is best. In some parts of the country, regrettably, the supply of pure spices for chili-making may not have kept pace with their growth in popularity. If you're stranded thus, fear not — you can order the spices by mail. (see page 90 for mail order sources). But what if you want to make chili *now* and your stock is depleted? You don't have time to "allow 4 to 6 weeks for delivery?"

31

In such a case I suggest a substitution rather than think about the consequences of chili deprivation. Go ahead, buy a commercial chili powder. For best results, buy one that has been tampered with least. In other words, one with few additives. From my experience the most unadulterated you will find is a chili powder consisting of chile, cumin, and oregano. Try to avoid ones with dried garlic and salt.

When using blended chili powder and working with a recipe that calls for pure ground chile and other spices, you have to try to adjust the quantities. Add up the total amount of ground chile, cumin, and oregano called for, then begin flavoring your chili with about half that amount of chili powder. Add seasonings until the chili tastes as you wish. For example, a recipe that calls for 3 tablespoons ground red chile, 2 teaspoons cumin and 1 teaspoon oregano totals up to 4 tablespoons of spices (3 teaspoons equal 1 tablespoon). So with chili powder you would begin by adding 2 tablespoons and progress slowly to four.

The reason I want you to start with less is so you can judge the quality and heat of the powder and then add more to suit. Let the flavors meld, then taste and add more until you're pleased with the taste.

**3.** If spices are the essence, the motivator, of chili, then the meat is the backbone. What you want is fresh beef in whatever cut the recipe calls for (if the recipe doesn't specify a cut, use lean chuck) coarsely chopped into about ¼- to ½-inch cubes — this is called "coarse chili grind." If other meats are used be sure to request the chili grind for them too. In the Southwestern U.S., you can buy chili grind beef in supermarkets. If you're making chili elsewhere ask the butcher to use a ½- to 1-inch blade in his meat grinder — the same blade used for making Italian sausage.

**4.** Once you have your essentials together, you're ready to begin cooking. Don't destroy your careful preparations with a haphazard approach. Believe me, I have seen haphazard in my time — especially at chili cookoffs where some contestants try to jazz up their act by tossing ingredients into the pot in alphabetic order, underhand from six feet away. Or hire gymnasts to do handsprings over the pot, adding ingredients from midair! Follow the instructions carefully, adding ingredients as they are called for and that includes the meat, vegetables (onions, green pepper, celery, tomatoes, for example), and spices.

**5.** Do *not* drain the grease from the pot either after you have browned the meat or at anytime during the cooking process. To skim is folly—you would rob the chili of its flavor. Fat is an important flavor catalyst for chili and should not be interfered with until the cooking is finished.

**6.** Simmering is vital to most chili recipes. It helps the flavors to get acquainted. Remember to leave the lid off the pot to let the juices cook down to a heavenly—and sometimes wicked—broth.

**7.** If you want beans in your chili, use freshly precooked ones. Don't put them in until the last half hour of cooking; if you cook them too long they'll go to mush and practically disappear!

**8.** When your brew has finished simmering, sample your endeavor (if you're like most chiliheads you'll have been doing so all along) and adjust the seasonings. If you've gone easy on the chile until this point and you decide to add more be sure to allow another half hour simmering time.

**9.** If your chili seems too greasy for your tastes you can now skim off some of the fat. For thorough and easy removal, after your chili is cooked, allow it to cool, refrigerate it for at least two to three hours and skim off the fat that has risen to the top.

**10.** Chili is a great convenience food; it improves with rest, age, and reheating, so try and make it a day in advance of serving. It also freezes well so always make enough for at least two meals.

And so, *amigo*, you have the essential elements . . . the methods to make this Chili Madness your slave, not your master!

**Cool Downs**

When you serve chili, always be ready to serve plenty of beverages. They'll disappear as fast as the food. Champagne, sangria (using red or white wine and plenty of orange and lemon slices), or a vigorous red wine—maybe a Zinfandel—are all delicious and good accompaniments to the muscular zing of your main dish. And so is beer. For a change of pace, serve Mexican beer, the south-of-the-border way. In Guadalajara, it is served icy cold in a lime juice-and-salt-rimmed can. For a bit more elegance, serve the beer in a goblet rimmed with the lime and salt. I call this a poor man's Margarita.

And speaking of Margaritas, while wine and beer are excellent with chili, a refreshing tequila-and-lime juice Margarita is *the* drink of choice, the perfect partner to your zesty dinner.

# Chili Cookoffs

It doesn't matter if you're a neophyte chili cook. Once your palate has been conditioned and chile peppers are circulating in your blood, chili may well become your life's sustenance. You'll start experimenting (as they say, there's always room for improvement)—adding a little more of this, substituting a little of that—until you create your own great chili, better known as your "masterpiece."

So then what? Your mother loves your concoction, your friends are beating your door down and turning into chili aficionados. "Is that all there is?" No! You can pit your labor of love and luck against others in a chili cookoff, the ultimate test.

A cookoff is, first and foremost, an incredible party among fellow chili lovers. (There is some intangible quality among people who love chili . . . sort of like a friendly port in a storm, a gathering of the chosen.) A cookoff is also a fierce competition between palates and cooking secrets, sometimes passed down for decades, sometimes a sudden whim. It is a no-holds-barred contest to pick the best darn tootin' chili around.

Formal chili cookoffs are held year-round throughout the country. They

**International Chili Society Cookoff winner, Nevada Annie (whose real name is LaVerne Harris), shows her grandson her prize-winning technique. For Nevada Annie's recipe, see page 69.**

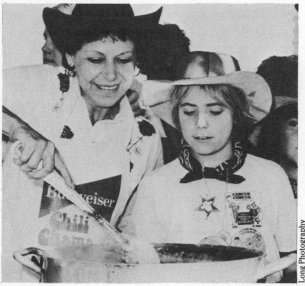

Long Photography
Courtesy of International Chili Society

Officially join the international chili community. The names and addresses of chili societies are supplied to help you get started.

begin with a series of local and statewide contests that culminate in large international events, carried out in compliance with carefully laid out guidelines. To find out if there's one such local contest within hiking, biking, or riding distance, write or even join one of the three organized associations:

Chile Appreciation Society, International, c/o Frank X. Tolbert
Tolbert's Original Texas Chili Parlor
3802 Cedar Springs
Dallas, Texas 75219

International Chili Society
P.O. Box 2966
Newport Beach, California 92663

International Connoisseurs of Green and
    Red Chile
World Headquarters
Box 3467
New Mexico State University
Las Cruces, New Mexico 88003

Each of these pod-loving groups publishes announcements of upcoming cookoffs, as well as newsletters of activities. Other reading materials include the popular fun-loving *Goat Gap Gazette* (c/o Wimberley, 5110 Bavard Lane, No. 2, Houston, Texas 77006; subscriptions cost $7.50 for eleven "ravishing, delectable" copies), which will keep you up on all the chili gossip.

If you're stranded in a chili wilderness — a community with no cookoffs — and want to be a trend setter, organize your own. If you're a newcomer to these events it is probably best to contact one of the societies. The International Chili Society, for one, goes so far as to sanction local contests — so you may wish to contact them. Even if you don't want to get totally involved, you may still want to write the ICS for their guidelines.

# Recipes for Chili Madness

# Pecos River Bowl of Red

Originally Pecos River was the name of the ranch I owned in New Mexico and now it is the name of the company I head. I developed this recipe around the line of pure ground chiles and other spices used in Mexican cooking that we produce. It follows the authentic tradition of Southwestern chili and has won the hearts of all my friends.

2 tablespoons lard, butter, or bacon
  drippings
1 large onion, coarsely chopped
3 pounds lean beef, coarse chili grind
3 medium cloves garlic, finely chopped
4 tablespoons ground hot red chile
4 tablespoons ground mild red chile
2 teaspoons ground cumin
3 cups water
1½ teaspoons salt

**1.** Melt the lard, butter, or drippings in a large heavy pot over medium heat. Add the onions and cook until they are translucent.

**2.** Combine the meat with the garlic, ground chile, and cumin. Add this meat-and-spice mixture to the pot. Break up any lumps with a fork and cook, stirring occasionally, until the meat is evenly browned.

**3.** Stir in the water and salt. Bring to a boil, then lower the heat and simmer, uncovered, for about 2½ to 3 hours, stirring occasionally, until the meat is very tender and the flavors are well blended. Add more water if necessary. Taste and adjust seasonings.

**Serves: 6**

# Jay's Chili

Jay Pennington became the International Chili Society's 1977 World Champion with this vegetable-meat version. It contains four kinds of peppers, including mild bell, and a chile salsa.

1 tablespoon cooking oil
3 medium onions, finely chopped
2 green bell peppers, cored, seeded, and finely chopped
2 stalks celery, finely chopped
3 medium cloves garlic, finely chopped
8 pounds beef round, coarse chili grind
2 20-ounce cans tomato sauce
2 20-ounce cans stewed tomatoes
1 6-ounce can tomato paste
5 cups water
1 4-ounce can chile salsa (see note)
1 3-inch canned, pickled jalapeño pepper, finely chopped
8 tablespoons ground hot red chile
4 tablespoons ground mild red chile
1 4-ounce can whole green chiles, seeded and finely chopped
1 tablespoon ground cumin
1 teaspoon dried oregano (preferably Mexican)
3 tablespoons salt
Freshly ground pepper to taste

**1.** Heat the oil in a heavy 10- to 12-quart pot over medium heat. Add the onions, bell peppers, celery, and garlic. Cook, stirring, until the onions are translucent.

**2.** Add the meat to the pot a little at a time, stirring occasionally, until the meat is evenly browned.

**3.** Stir in the remaining ingredients. Bring to a boil, then lower heat and simmer, uncovered, for 2½ to 3 hours. Stir often. Taste and adjust seasonings.

**Serves: 16**

Note: Chile salsa is a relish made from equal parts of finely chopped raw onion, tomatoes (peeled, cored, seeded, and finely chopped) and canned chopped green or pickled jalapeño chiles. It is widely available in supermarkets and specialty foods stores.

# Santa Clara Chili

Pueblo Indians in Santa Clara, New Mexico were perhaps the first chile-pepper aficionados. They were enjoying the pepper pod centuries before the Spanish arrived in the sixteenth century.

3    tablespoons lard
2    pounds lean beef chuck, cut into ½-inch cubes
3    tablespoons flour in a paper bag
1    medium onion, coarsely chopped
2    medium cloves garlic, finely chopped
5    tablespoons ground hot red chile
3    tablespoons ground mild red chile
1½   teaspoons salt
½    teaspoon dried oregano (preferably Mexican)
     Pinch ground cumin
4    cups beef broth
6    cups stewed pinto beans, fresh or canned

**1.** Melt the lard in a large heavy skillet over medium heat. Coat cubes with flour by shaking them in the paper bag with the flour. Add cubes to the skillet, stirring to brown evenly.

**2.** Add the onion and garlic and cook until the onion is translucent.

**3.** Remove from the heat and stir in the ground chile, coating the beef-and-onion mixture evenly. Add the remaining seasonings and stir, then add a small amount of broth. Over low heat cook, stirring, until the mixture is smooth and thick. Continue to add broth a little at a time, stirring, until all is added. Cook, uncovered, for 1 to 2 hours.

**4.** Serve with a dish of stewed pinto beans. Traditionally the beans are topped with the chili mixture.

**Serves: 6**

# Craig Claiborne's No-Salt Chili con Carne

When Craig Claiborne, well-known chef and cookbook author, was put on a no-salt diet he had two ultimate cravings: one was for a good hamburger and the other for a good bowl of chili. He developed this recipe in which the lack of salt is compensated for by the cumin, garlic, and a touch of red wine vinegar.

| | |
|---|---|
| 1 | tablespoon peanut or vegetable oil |
| 3 | medium onions, finely chopped |
| 1 | green bell or sweet red pepper, cored, seeded, and finely chopped |
| 1¼ | pounds veal, beef, or pork, coarse chili grind |
| 2 | medium cloves garlic, finely chopped |
| 2 | tablespoons ground hot red chile |
| 1 | tablespoon ground mild red chile |
| 1 | teaspoon ground cumin |
| 1 | teaspoon dried oregano (preferably Mexican) |
| 1 | bay leaf |
| ½ | teaspoon freshly ground black pepper |
| 4 | cups fresh or canned unsalted tomatoes |
| 1 | tablespoon red wine vinegar |
| ¼ | teaspoon chile caribe, or to taste (see page 26) |

**1.** Heat the oil in a deep skillet over medium heat. Add the onions and green pepper and sauté until the onions are translucent, about 3 minutes.

**2.** Sprinkle the meat with the garlic, ground chile, cumin, and oregano. Stir to blend. Add the meat to the skillet. Break up any lumps with a fork, stirring occasionally until the meat is evenly browned.

**3.** Add the bay leaf, pepper, tomatoes, vinegar, and caribe. Bring to a boil, lower the heat and simmer 1 hour, stirring occasionally. Taste and adjust seasoning.

**Serves: 2**

# Reno Red

An International Chili Society World Championship Cookoff winner in 1979, this recipe was devised by Joe and Shirley Stewart. The added touches of oregano-flavored beer, cider vinegar, and mashed dried chile pods make this recipe particularly hearty and different.

1 cup kidney suet or cooking oil
3 pounds beef round, coarse chili grind
3 pounds beef chuck, coarse chili grind
   Whole black peppercorns, crushed
12 tablespoons ground red chile (hot, mild, or a combination of both, to taste)
6 tablespoons ground cumin
6 small cloves garlic, finely chopped
2 medium onions, coarsely chopped
   Water
6 dried whole red chiles, crushed, or ¾ cup chile caribe (see page 26)
1 tablespoon dried oregano (preferably Mexican) brewed like tea in ½ cup warm beer (room temperature)
2 tablespoons paprika
2 tablespoons cider vinegar
3 cups beef broth
1 4-ounce can diced green chiles, drained
1 4-ounce can stewed tomatoes
1 teaspoon liquid hot pepper sauce
2 tablespoons masa harina (corn flour)

1. Melt the suet or heat the cooking oil in a large heavy pot over medium-high heat. Add the meat and the black pepper to taste, to the pot. Break up any lumps with a fork and cook, stirring occasionally, until the meat is evenly browned.

2. Stir in the ground chile, cumin, garlic, and onions. Add a small amount of water to barely cover. Bring to a boil, then lower the heat and simmer, uncovered, for 30 to 45 minutes, adding water as necessary.

3. Stir the crushed red chiles into the meat mixture. Strain the oregano-beer "tea" and stir the liquid into the pot. Discard the oregano. Stir in the paprika, vinegar, 2 cups of beef broth, diced chiles, tomatoes, and hot pepper sauce. Simmer, uncovered, for 30 to 45 minutes longer. Stir often.

4. Dissolve the masa flour in the remaining 1 cup of broth. Stir it into the pot and simmer, uncovered, ½ hour longer.

**Serves: 12**

# New Mexican Chili Pork

It is not unusual to use pork in a chili recipe. This meat creates a sweeter-flavored dish. The pinto beans are served on the side or with the chili ladled over them in the typical New Mexican style. For tradition's sake—to say nothing of great flavor—accompany the meal with hot tortillas and honey.

---

3 pounds pork shoulder, fat and bone removed, cut into ½-inch cubes (reserve fat)
1 teaspoon salt
2 medium cloves garlic, finely chopped
8 tablespoons ground mild red chile (add part ground hot red chile if desired)
½ teaspoon dried oregano (preferably Mexican)
3 cups chicken broth
4 cups freshly stewed pinto beans (or 2 16-ounce cans)

**1.** Melt the pork fat in a heavy skillet over medium-high heat. Add the pork cubes a few at a time, stirring to brown evenly.

**2.** Add the salt and garlic, stirring well. Remove from the heat and stir in the ground chile and oregano, coating the meat evenly with the spices. (If you are using a combination of mild and hot chile, do not add the hot spice yet.) Add a small amount of broth and stir well.

**3.** Return to the heat, add a bit more broth and stir. Continue to add broth, a little at a time, stirring, until the chili is smooth, then reduce the heat and simmer, uncovered, for about 1 hour.

**4.** Taste and adjust seasonings adding the ground hot chile to taste at this point. To add, remove the pot from the heat, sprinkle the chile over the top, and stir well.

**5.** Serve the chili with a bowl of freshly stewed pinto beans on the side.

**Serves: 6 to 8**

# Pedernales River Chili

Reported to have been Lyndon B. Johnson's favorite, this recipe comes from deep in the heart of Texas.

3  tablespoons lard or bacon drippings
4  pounds lean beef, coarse chili grind
1  large onion, coarsely chopped
2  medium cloves garlic, finely chopped
3  teaspoons salt
1  teaspoon dried oregano (preferably Mexican)
1  teaspoon ground cumin
2  cups boiling water
1  32-ounce can whole tomatoes
4  tablespoons ground hot red chile
2  tablespoons ground mild red chile

**1.** Melt the lard or bacon drippings in a large sauté pan over medium-high heat. Add the meat to the pan. Break up any lumps with a fork and cook, stirring occasionally until the meat is evenly browned.

**2.** Add the onions and garlic and cook until the onions are translucent.

**3.** Stir in the salt, oregano, cumin, water, and tomatoes.

**4.** Gradually stir in the ground chile, testing until you achieve the degree of hotness and flavor that suits your palate. Bring to a boil, then lower heat and simmer, uncovered, for 1 hour. Stir occasionally.

**Serves: 8**

# Amarillo Chili

A marriage of pork and beef create a full-flavored chili fiesta.

| | |
|---|---|
| 4 | slices bacon, cut into ½-inch pieces |
| 2 | medium onions, coarsely chopped |
| 1 | medium clove garlic, finely chopped |
| ½ | pound lean pork shoulder, coarse chili grind |
| 1 | pound beef round, cut into ½-inch strips |
| ½ | pound beef chuck, coarse chili grind |
| 4 | canned whole green chiles, seeded and chopped |
| 1 | tablespoon ground hot red chile |
| 2 | tablespoons ground mild red chile |
| 1 | teaspoon dried oregano (preferably Mexican) |
| 1½ | teaspoons ground cumin |
| 1½ | teaspoons salt |
| 2 | 6-ounce cans tomato paste |
| 3 | cups water |
| 1 | 16-ounce can pinto beans, drained |

1. Fry bacon in a large, deep, heavy pot over medium heat. When the bacon has rendered most of its fat, remove the pieces with a slotted spoon, drain on paper toweling and reserve.

2. Add the onions and garlic to the bacon fat and cook until the onions are translucent.

3. Add the pork and beef to the pot. Break up any lumps with a fork and cook over medium-high heat, stirring occasionally, until the meat is evenly browned.

4. Stir in all the remaining ingredients except the beans and the bacon. Bring to a boil, then lower the heat and simmer, uncovered, for 2 hours. Stir occasionally.

5. Taste and adjust seasonings. Stir in the beans and the bacon, and simmer for ½ hour longer.

**Serves: 4**

# Midwest Chili

Easy to prepare, this chili recipe calls for a combination of coarsely ground and finely ground meat giving the finished product a nice texture. You might like to substitute butter beans for the pinto beans as some Midwesterners do.

---

3   pounds beef chuck, coarse chili grind
2   pounds beef chuck, hamburger grind
2   large onions, coarsely chopped
5   medium cloves garlic, finely chopped
1   tablespoon ground hot red chile
5   tablespoons ground mild red chile
3   tablespoons ground cumin
3   teaspoons salt
3   cups water
2   15-ounce cans tomato sauce
2   28-ounce cans peeled whole tomatoes
4   cups freshly cooked pinto beans, drained (or 2 16-ounce cans)

**1.** Add the meat, onions, and garlic to a heavy 5-quart pot or Dutch oven. Break up any lumps with a fork and cook over medium heat, stirring occasionally, until the meat is evenly browned.

**2.** Stir in the ground chile, cumin, and salt, thoroughly blending the mixture. Add the water, tomato sauce, and tomatoes, mashing them with a fork.

**3.** Bring the mixture to a boil, then lower the heat and simmer, uncovered, for about 1½ hours. Stir occasionally.

**4.** Taste and adjust seasonings. Stir in the beans and simmer, uncovered, ½ hour longer.

**Serves: 10 to 12**

# Chili H. Allen Smith

With this recipe, H. Allen Smith, humorist, writer, Easterner, and disrespecter of Texas-style chili, entered the first chili cookoff ever held. Sponsored by the Chili Appreciation Society, International (CASI) and held in Terlingua, Texas, in 1967, the contest between Smith and Wick Fowler, a Texan and CASI chief cook, ended in a tie.

2  tablespoons olive oil or butter
4  pounds beef sirloin or tenderloin, coarse chili grind
1  6-ounce can tomato paste
4  cups water
3  medium onions, coarsely chopped
1  green bell pepper, cored, seeded and coarsely chopped
4  large cloves garlic, finely chopped
3  tablespoons ground hot red chile
1  tablespoon dried oregano (preferably Mexican)
½  teaspoon dried basil
1  tablespoon cumin seed or ground cumin
   Salt and freshly ground pepper to taste

**1.** Heat the oil or butter (or a blend of the two) in a heavy 4-quart pot over medium heat. Add the meat to the pot. Break up any lumps with a fork and cook, stirring occasionally, until the meat is evenly browned.

**2.** Stir in the remaining ingredients. Bring to a boil, then lower heat and simmer, uncovered, for 2 to 3 hours. Stir occasionally and add more water if necessary. Taste and adjust seasoning.

**Serves: 8**

# Chili Woody DeSilva

2 tablespoons cooking oil
5 medium onions, coarsely chopped
Salt and freshly ground pepper to taste
4 pounds beef chuck, coarse chili grind
5 medium cloves garlic, finely chopped
4 tablespoons dried oregano (preferably
Mexican)
2 teaspoons woodruff
1 tablespoon ground hot red chile
1 teaspoon cayenne pepper
2 tablespoons paprika
3 tablespoons ground cumin
Scant teaspoon to 1 teaspoon chipeños
(pequin chiles), crushed
4 dashes liquid hot pepper sauce
3 10-ounce cans tomato sauce
1 6-ounce can tomato paste
Water
4 tablespoons masa harina or all-
purpose flour

A super-spicy stew with an extra touch—woodruff. It may not be easy to find this herb but try your local specialty food stores or H. Roth and Son in New York (see Mail Order Sources, page 90). This recipe calls for the chili to be made a day in advance, with the masa harina (corn flour) or thickening added just before serving.

**1.** Heat the oil in a large heavy skillet over medium heat. Add the onions. Season with salt and pepper and cook, stirring, until the onions are translucent. Remove to a large heavy pot.

**2.** Add the meat to the skillet, pouring in more oil if necessary. Add garlic and 1 tablespoon of the oregano. Break up any lumps with a fork and cook over medium-high heat, stirring occasionally, until the meat is evenly browned. Add this mixture to the pot.

**3.** In a small plastic or paper bag, shake together the remaining 3 tablespoons of oregano, the woodruff, ground chile, cayenne pepper, paprika, cumin, and the chipeños. Add the blended spices to the pot as well as the liquid hot pepper sauce, tomato sauce, and tomato paste.

**4.** Add enough water to cover. Bring to a boil, then lower the heat and simmer, uncovered, for at least 2 hours. Taste and adjust seasonings.

**5.** Cool the chili and refrigerate it overnight. The next day, skim off the excess fat. Reheat the chili to the boiling point and stir in a paste made of the masa harina and a little water. Stir constantly to prevent sticking and scorching, adding water as necessary for the desired texture.

**Serves: 8**

# Carroll Shelby's Chili

This recipe is the coup de grace of Grand Prix racer Carroll Shelby but if you use hot chile pepper in the amount called for, beware! It is truly a pot of fire. Best to start off with less and add more to taste while the chili is cooking.

½ pound suet or ½ cup cooking oil
1 pound beef round, coarse chili grind
1 pound beef chuck, coarse chili grind
1 8-ounce can tomato sauce
1 12-ounce can beer
¼ cup ground hot red chile
2 medium cloves garlic, finely chopped
1 small onion, finely chopped
1¼ teaspoons dried oregano (preferably Mexican)
  Scant ½ teaspoon paprika
1½ teaspoons ground cumin
1¼ teaspoons salt
  Pinch cayenne pepper
¾ pound Monterey Jack cheese, grated

1. Melt the suet or heat the oil in a heavy 3-quart (or larger) pot over medium-high heat. Remove the unrendered suet and add the meat to the pot. Break up any lumps with a fork and cook, stirring occasionally, until the meat is evenly browned.

2. Add the tomato sauce, beer, ground chile, garlic, onion, oregano, paprika, 1 teaspoon of the cumin, and the salt. Stir to blend. Bring to a boil, then lower the heat and simmer, uncovered, for 1 hour. Stir occasionally.

3. Taste and adjust seasonings, adding the cayenne pepper. Simmer, uncovered, 1 hour longer.

4. Stir in the cheese and the remaining ½ teaspoon of the cumin. Simmer ½ hour longer, stirring often to keep the cheese from burning.

**Serves: 4**

# Chocolaty Chili

From the company that brought you those great chocolate chips—Nestlé. Chocolate added to the mixture creates a Mexican molé-like flavor.

2   tablespoons vegetable oil
1   medium onion, finely chopped
2   cloves garlic, finely chopped
1   pound lean beef, coarse chili grind
1   16-ounce can kidney beans, drained
1   16-ounce can tomato puree
1   6-ounce can tomato paste
½   cup fresh whole domestic green chiles (approximately 4), parched, peeled, seeded, and chopped (see page 26)
½   cup water
2   ounces bittersweet chocolate, in 1 ounce pieces
2   tablespoons ground red chile (hot, mild, or a combination of both to taste)
1   teaspoon ground cumin
1   beef bouillon cube

**1.** Heat the oil in a large skillet over medium heat. Add the onion and garlic and cook until the onion is translucent.

**2.** Add the meat to the skillet. Break up any lumps with a fork and cook, stirring occasionally, until the meat is evenly browned.

**3.** Stir in the kidney beans, tomato puree, tomato paste, green chile, water, 1 ounce of the chocolate, ground chile, cumin and beef cube. Mix well. Bring to a boil, then lower heat and simmer, uncovered, for ½ hour. Stir occasionally.

**4.** Stir in the remaining chocolate and continue cooking until it is thoroughly blended. Taste and adjust seasonings.

**Serves: 2**

# Mike Roy's Housebroken Chili

1½  tablespoons lard or bacon drippings
1   medium onion, coarsely chopped
1   medium clove garlic, finely chopped
1   tablespoon orange rind, grated
2   pounds lean beef (preferably shank),
        coarse chili grind
3   tablespoons ground hot red chile
1   tablespoon ground mild red chile
1   tablespoon ground cumin
1   tablespoon salt
½   teaspoon freshly ground black
        pepper
2   cups water
1   cup beef broth
3   tablespoons orange-flavored liqueur
1   teaspoon liquid hot pepper sauce

Tamed by a zesty orange "twist," from the addition of orange rind and liqueur, this sophisticated recipe got the nickname of "housebroken."

**1.** Melt the lard or bacon drippings in a large heavy skillet over medium-high heat. Add the onion, garlic, and orange rind and cook until the onion is translucent.

**2.** Add the beef to the skillet. Break up any lumps with a fork and cook, stirring occasionally, until the meat is evenly browned.

**3.** Stir in the ground chile, cumin, salt, pepper, water, and broth. Bring to a boil, then lower the heat and simmer, uncovered, for 3 to 4 hours. Stir occasionally and add water if necessary.

**4.** Add the liqueur and hot pepper sauce. Taste, adjust seasonings and cook, uncovered, for 15 minutes longer.

**Serves: 4**

# First-Love Chili

This recipe is highly recommended for a chili newcomer. It has been known to warm the cockles of the heart and secure a long-lasting devotion. The cinnamon and cloves add a particularly nice flavor but remember to remove them before serving. Although the proportions listed produce a chili-for-two (enough for one chili devotee plus one novice), they can be easily doubled to serve four.

1   tablespoon lard
1   large onion, finely chopped
2   medium cloves garlic, finely chopped
1   pound lean beef, coarse chili grind
2   tablespoons ground red chile (hot or mild or a combination to taste)
1   teaspoon celery salt
¼   teaspoon cayenne pepper
1   teaspoon ground cumin
½   teaspoon dried basil
1   teaspoon salt
1   16-ounce can plum tomatoes
1   small bay leaf
3   cups water
1   small cinnamon stick
2   whole cloves
1   green bell pepper, cored, seeded, and coarsely chopped
1   16-ounce can kidney beans

**1.** Melt the lard in a large heavy pot over medium-high heat. Add the onion and garlic and cook until the onion is translucent.

**2.** Add the meat to the pot. Break up any lumps with a fork and cook, stirring occasionally, until the meat is evenly browned.

**3.** Stir in the remaining ingredients up through the cloves. Bring to a boil, then lower the heat and simmer, uncovered, for 2½ hours. Stir occasionally.

**4.** Stir in the green pepper and kidney beans and simmer, uncovered, for ½ hour longer.

**5.** Remove the cinnamon stick, bay leaf and, if possible, the cloves. Taste and adjust seasonings.

**Serves: 2**

# Murray's Girlfriend's Cincinnati Chili

Don Singleton, a food reporter for the New York *Daily News* discovered Cincinnati folks to be enthusiastic "chili mavens." He gives this spicy specialty a "six-Rolaid" rating.

2   tablespoons butter
2   pounds beef, hamburger grind
6   bay leaves
1   large onion, finely chopped
6   medium cloves garlic, finely chopped
1   teaspoon cinnamon
2   teaspoons allspice
4   teaspoons vinegar
1   teaspoon dried whole red pepper, crushed or chile caribe (see page 26)
1½  teaspoons salt
2   tablespoons pure ground red chile (hot, mild, or a combination of both, to taste)
1   teaspoon ground cumin
½   teaspoon dried oregano (preferably Mexican)
1   6-ounce can tomato paste
6   cups water
1   16-ounce can kidney beans, drained
½   pound vermicelli, cooked according to package directions
½   cup cheddar cheese, grated
1   small onion, finely chopped

**1.** Heat the butter in a large heavy skillet over medium-high heat. Add the meat to the skillet. Break up any lumps with a fork and cook, stirring occasionally, until the meat is evenly browned.

**2.** Stir in all the remaining ingredients up through the water. Taste and adjust seasonings. If the flavor is too sweet, add a small amount of vinegar; if not spicy enough, add a small amount of ground chile.

**3.** Bring the mixture to a boil, then lower the heat and simmer, uncovered, for 2 to 4 hours. Add the kidney beans to the mixture ½ hour before serving.

**4.** Place a small amount of the cooked vermicelli in individual bowls. Spoon on a generous amount of chili. Top with grated cheese and raw onion or pass in individual bowls.

**Serves: 6**

# Gringo Chili

This easy recipe makes up into a mild chili and in bigger batches is particularly good for children's parties. A great change from the usual fare, a child can probably prepare it him or herself (with some assistance).

---

2 teaspoons lard, butter, or bacon drippings
½ medium onion, coarsely chopped
1 pound lean beef round, coarse chili grind
2 tablespoons ground hot red chile
1 tablespoon ground mild red chile
¾ teaspoon dried oregano (preferably Mexican)
¾ teaspoon ground cumin
2 medium cloves garlic, finely chopped
2 10½-ounce cans tomato soup
1 10½-ounce can onion soup
2 16-ounce cans kidney beans, drained

**1.** Melt the lard, butter, or drippings in a large heavy pot over medium heat. Add the onion and cook until it is translucent.

**2.** Combine the meat with the ground chile, oregano, cumin, and garlic. Add this meat-and-spice mixture to the pot. Break up any lumps with a fork and cook, stirring occasionally, until the meat is evenly browned.

**3.** Stir in the tomato soup, onion soup, and beans. Bring to a boil, then lower the heat and simmer, uncovered, for ½ hour until the liquids cook down and the mixture thickens. Taste and adjust seasonings.

**Serves: 4**

# Esquire Fortnightly's Eastern Establishment Chili

| | | | |
|---|---|---|---|
| 2 | cups dried kidney beans | 1 | tablespoon chile caribe (see page 26) |
| ⅓ | cup olive oil or lard | 2 | tablespoons ground cumin |
| 5 | pounds beef brisket, cut into ½-inch cubes | 2 | tablespoons masa harina (corn flour) |
| 2 | large onions, coarsely chopped | 6 | cups canned tomatoes, chopped, reserve liquid |
| 6 | large cloves garlic, finely chopped | ½ | cup freshly brewed coffee |
| 2 | green bell peppers, cored, seeded, and coarsely chopped | | Salt and freshly ground black pepper |
| 2 | tablespoons dried basil | | |
| 1 | bay leaf | | |
| 2 | tablespoons ground mild red chile | | |
| 1 | tablespoon cayenne pepper | | |

Pecos River Spice Company's chile seasonings were first introduced in *Esquire* magazine's winning brew—at a 1979 chili cookoff held at Bloomingdale's in New York City that pitted a cook from the East representing *Esquire* against a Texan from *Texas Monthly* magazine.

Although the recipe *Esquire* used is definitely an Easterner's version of chili—not a traditional Western brew—the flavor is terrific.

**1.** Place the beans in a bowl, cover with water and soak overnight.

**2.** Pour the beans and the water in which they were soaked into a heavy saucepan. Bring to a boil over high heat, then lower the heat and simmer, covered, for about 1 hour or until tender. Stir occasionally.

**3.** Heat the oil or melt the lard in a large heavy casserole over medium heat. Pat the brisket dry and add it to the casserole. Stir the beef often until it is quite brown on all sides. Remove it from the casserole and set aside.

**4.** Add more oil or lard to the casserole if needed, then add the onions and garlic and cook until the onions are translucent. Stir in the green peppers, basil, bay leaf, ground chile, cayenne pepper, caribe, and cumin. Cook for about 1 minute, then add the masa harina and cook 1 or 2 minutes longer.

**5.** Return the brisket to the casserole and add the tomatoes and their liquid. Bring to a boil, then lower the heat and simmer, uncovered, for 2 hours. Stir occasionally.

**6.** Stir in the salt and black pepper. Taste and adjust seasonings. Add the coffee and simmer, uncovered, for 1 hour longer.

**7.** Add the kidney beans to the chili. Simmer, uncovered, for another ½ hour.

**Serves: 10**

# Jeanne Owen's Chili con Carne

⅓  cup olive oil
3  pounds lean beef round, cut into
    1-inch cubes
2  medium onions, finely chopped
3  medium cloves garlic, finely
    chopped
   Salt
4  cups boiling water
1  teaspoon caraway seeds
2  teaspoons sesame seeds
½  teaspoon ground oregano
    (preferably Mexican)
2  to 4 tablespoons ground red chile
    (hot or mild or a combination)
1  cup pitted green olives
2  16-ounce cans kidney beans,
    drained

Sesame, caraway seeds, and olives create a unique flavor in this brew. Still very much chili, the nutty taste surprisingly brings to mind Europe and a Bavarian Oktoberfest. A perfect dish to sit down to sometime in the autumn — maybe after raking the leaves.

1. Heat the oil in a large sauté pan or 6-quart braising pan over medium heat. Add the beef cubes a few at a time, stirring to brown evenly. As they are browned, remove cubes to a plate and set aside, add more cubes to the pan. Continue the process, adding more oil if necessary, until all the meat is browned.

2. Add the onions to the pan and cook, stirring, for a few minutes, then add the garlic. Cook until the onions are translucent.

3. Return the beef cubes to the pan, season with salt to taste, then add the boiling water, caraway and sesame seeds, and oregano. Bring to a boil, then lower the heat and simmer, covered, for 1 hour.

4. Gradually stir in the ground chile, tasting until you achieve the degree of hotness and flavor that suits your palate.

5. Add the olives and simmer, covered, 1 hour longer.

6. Taste and adjust seasonings, then mix in the kidney beans and heat through.

**Serves: 6**

# Buzzard's Breath Chili

Have some fun with this one. The original version calls for "dead cow meat," dried red ants, and cigar ashes. Well . . . you decide. It will probably be quite at home in your kitchen and without the insects or ash. Still, this recipe, everything included, took first prize at the Chili Appreciation Society, International Cookoff in Terlingua, Texas, in 1971.

3   tablespoons lard, butter, or bacon
      drippings
2   large onions, coarsely chopped
8   pounds beef chuck or round, coarse
      chili grind
5   cloves garlic, finely chopped
5   tablespoons, plus 1 teaspoon ground
      hot red chile
5   tablespoons, plus 1 teaspoon ground
      mild red chile
1   tablespoon cumin
1   teaspoon dried oregano (preferably
      Mexican)
3   8-ounce cans tomato sauce
3   cups water
2   tablespoons salt
      Parsley (optional)
1   cup masa harina (corn flour)

**1.** Melt the lard, butter, or drippings in a large heavy pot over medium heat. Add the onions and cook until they are translucent.

**2.** Combine the beef with the garlic, ground chile, cumin, and oregano. Add this meat-and-spice mixture to the pot with the onions. Break up any lumps with a fork and cook, stirring occasionally about ½ hour, until the meat is evenly browned.

**3.** Add the tomato sauce, water, salt, and optional parsley. Bring to a boil, then lower the heat and simmer, uncovered, for 1 hour.

**4.** Stir in the masa harina to achieve the desired consistency.

**5.** Cook 10 minutes longer, stirring. Taste and adjust seasonings.

**Serves: 16**

# Cookout Chili

**Charbroiling the meat and roasting the peppers over an open fire adds a real outdoors taste to this wildly hot chili.**

1 pound beef chuck, hamburger grind
1 green bell pepper, cored, seeded, and halved
4 fresh whole domestic green chiles
1 fresh or canned, pickled jalapeño pepper
2 scallions, including tops, coarsely chopped
1 16-ounce can tomato sauce
½ teaspoon dried oregano (preferably Mexican)
½ teaspoon ground cumin
1 teaspoon ground hot red chile
1 teaspoon chile caribe (see page 26)
1 16-ounce can kidney beans

**1.** Form the meat into three or four hamburger patties.

**2.** Over a grill, charcoal broil the hamburgers until they are medium rare on the inside and nicely crisp on the outside. Set them aside to cool.

**3.** Lightly roast the bell pepper, green chiles and jalapeño (if fresh) over the fire. Peel and prepare the roasted green chiles according to the directions on page 26, then finely chop all the peppers.

**4.** Crumble the hamburgers into a large skillet or Dutch oven and add the peppers and the remaining ingredients to the meat. Simmer over the fire for at least 30 minutes. Stir occasionally. Taste and adjust seasonings.

**Serves: 2**

# Texas/Two Fingers Chili

2  tablespoons vegetable oil
3  pounds lean beef, coarse chili grind
2  medium cloves garlic, finely chopped
5  tablespoons ground mild red chile
1  tablespoon ground cumin
1½  teaspoons cayenne pepper
1  tablespoon dried oregano (preferably Mexican)
1  tablespoon salt
2  cups tequila
6  cups water

½  cup masa harina (corn flour)
1  dried whole red chile, crushed, or 2 tablespoons chile caribe (optional, see page 26)
1  teaspoon liquid hot pepper sauce (optional)

Given to me at the San Francisco Pillsbury Bakeoff a few years ago, I cooked up the recipe and liked the unusual taste. Tequila seems to impart a subtle tang that most brews don't possess. Obviously, the recipe was prepared to promote a brand of tequila—Two Fingers—hence the name.

**1.** Heat the oil in a large heavy pot over medium-high heat. Add the meat to the pot. Break up any lumps with a fork and cook, stirring occasionally, until the meat is evenly browned.

**2.** Stir in the garlic, ground chile, cumin, cayenne pepper, oregano, salt, tequila, water, and masa harina. Bring to a boil, then lower the heat and simmer, uncovered, for about 1½ hours.

**3.** Taste and adjust seasonings. If desired, add the crushed chile pepper and the optional hot pepper sauce and simmer, uncovered, for ½ hour longer.

**Serves: 6**

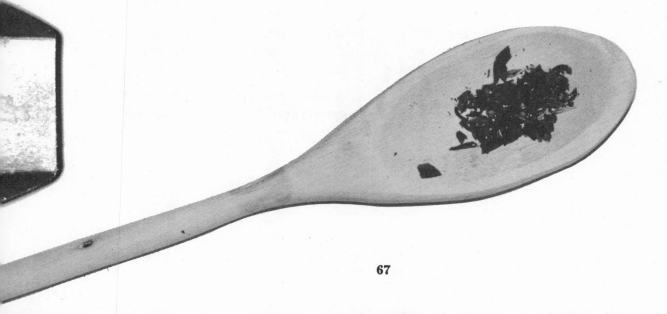

# Diet Chili

On a waist-trimming regimen? If so, you can still enjoy that terrific chili taste and get only 247 calories in each one-cup serving of this good savory stew.

1 tablespoon vegetable oil
2 medium onions, finely chopped
2 pounds lean beef, coarse chili grind
2 tablespoons ground hot red chile
3 tablespoons ground mild red chile
1 medium clove garlic, crushed
1 teaspoon dried oregano (preferably Mexican)
1½ teaspoons cumin
½ teaspoon salt
4 or 5 tomatoes, peeled, cored, seeded, and coarsely chopped
3 4-ounce cans whole green chiles, seeded and chopped, reserve liquid

1. Heat the oil in a medium-sized heavy saucepan over medium heat. Add the onions and cook until they are translucent.

2. Combine the meat with the ground chile, garlic, oregano, cumin, and salt. Add this meat-and-spice mixture to the pan. Break up any lumps with a fork and cook, stirring occasionally, about 15 minutes until the meat is evenly browned.

3. Add the tomatoes and green chiles with their liquid. Bring to a boil, then lower the heat and simmer, uncovered, for 1 hour. Stir occasionally, adding water if necessary. Taste and adjust seasonings.

4. Allow to cool, then refrigerate. When fat has risen and congealed, skim it off, then reheat chile.

**Serves: 8**

# Nevada Annie's Cowboy Chili

LaVerne Harris, a.k.a. Nevada Annie, became the 1978 World Champion at the International Chili Society Cookoff with this delicious recipe. Her special advice to the cook is to be sure to add in the most important ingredient—"lots of love."

½ cup lard
3 medium onions, coarsely chopped
2 green bell peppers, cored, seeded, and coarsely chopped
2 stalks celery, coarsely chopped
1 tablespoon canned, pickled jalapeño peppers (approximately 2 peppers), finely chopped
8 pounds beef chuck, coarse chili grind
2 15-ounce cans stewed tomatoes
1 15-ounce can tomato sauce with mushrooms
1 6-ounce can tomato paste
8 tablespoons ground hot red chile
4 tablespoons ground mild red chile
2 teaspoons ground cumin
3 bay leaves
1 tablespoon liquid hot pepper sauce
Garlic salt to taste
Onion salt to taste
Salt and freshly ground pepper to taste
4 ounces beer
Water

**1.** Heat the lard in a large heavy pot over medium-high heat. Add the onions, peppers, celery, and jalapeños. Cook, stirring, until the onions are translucent.

**2.** Add the meat to the pot. Break up any lumps with a fork and cook, stirring occasionally, until the meat is evenly browned.

**3.** Stir in the remaining ingredients with enough water to cover. Bring to a boil, then lower the heat and simmer, uncovered, for 3 hours. Stir often. Taste and adjust seasonings.

**Serves: 16**

# Navajo Green Chili

Novices are too green for this chili. It is a favorite of the Navajos and they like it cooked hot. Go light on the peppers when starting out; you can always add more.

3  pounds pork shoulder, fat and bone removed, cut into ½-inch cubes (reserve fat)
⅓  cup flour in a heavy paper bag
3  medium onions, coarsely chopped
4  medium cloves garlic, finely chopped
2  16-ounce cans whole green chiles, drained, seeded and cut into 2-inch slices
2  16-ounce cans whole tomatoes
1  6-ounce can tomato paste
3  cups water
2½  teaspoons salt
½  teaspoon dried oregano (preferably Mexican)

**1.** Melt the pork fat in a heavy skillet over medium-high heat. Coat the pork cubes with flour by shaking them in the paper bag with the flour. Add the cubes to the skillet a few at a time, stirring to brown evenly. Remove the cubes to a 5-quart Dutch oven or other heavy pot. Continue browning the pork cubes in the skillet until all are browned.

**2.** Add the onions and garlic to the skillet. Cook, stirring occasionally, until the onions are translucent. Add to the pot with the pork.

**3.** Stir the remaining ingredients into the pork-and-onion mixture. Bring to a boil, then lower the heat and simmer, uncovered, for ½ hour. Taste, adjust seasonings and cook for ½ hour longer.

**Serves: 6**

# Dallas Chili

Straight from Big D . . . and from a very proud chef who modestly claims it's the world's greatest. It is unusual, containing no onions but instead ingredients like gumbo filé and chicken fat not ordinarily associated with chili. Try it sometime when you're in an exotic mood. This brew simmers for a total of 12 hours.

6 pounds beef brisket, coarse chili grind
4 tablespoons ground hot red chile
1 tablespoon ground mild red chile
½ tablespoon chili caribe (see page 26)
1 teaspoon cayenne pepper
2 tablespoons dried oregano (preferably Mexican)
8 medium cloves garlic, crushed
4 bay leaves, crushed
1 teaspoon gumbo filé (ground sassafras)
3 tablespoons ground cumin
3 tablespoons woodruff* or 2 ounces unsweetened chocolate
1 teaspoon paprika
1 tablespoon salt
⅓ cup bacon drippings
2 tablespoons lemon juice
2 tablespoons lime juice
1 tablespoon Dijon mustard
2 tablespoons masa harina (corn flour)
4 12-ounce cans beer
1 tablespoon Worcestershire sauce
1 tablespoon sugar
1 tablespoon chicken fat (optional)
  Liquid hot pepper sauce (optional)

1. Combine the beef with the ground chile, caribe, cayenne pepper, oregano, garlic, bay leaves, gumbo filé, cumin, woodruff (if used), paprika, and salt.

2. Heat the bacon drippings in a large heavy pot over medium heat. Add the meat-and-spice mixture to the pot. Break up any lumps with a fork and cook, stirring occasionally, until the meat is evenly browned.

3. Stir in the remaining ingredients (including the chocolate, if used, and the optional chicken fat and liquid hot pepper sauce). Bring to a boil, then lower the heat and simmer, uncovered, for 2 hours. Taste and adjust seasonings.

4. Simmer, uncovered, for 10 hours longer, adding more beer or water and stirring as needed. Skim off fat before serving.

**Serves: 12**

*See H. Roth and Son under Mail Order Sources, page 90.

71

# Sun Dance Chili

Straight from Scottsdale, Arizona—real sun country—where the sun dance is a popular Indian art motif. This "veggie" brew is a subtle version appealing to those who don't like chili too hot or too pure!

2 tablespoons lard, butter, or bacon drippings
1 large onion, coarsely chopped
½ stalk celery, finely chopped
1 bell pepper, finely chopped
½ cup fresh sliced mushrooms
3 pounds beef, coarse chili grind
2 tablespoons ground hot red chile
1 tablespoon ground mild red chile
½ teaspoon dried oregano (preferably Mexican)
1 teaspoon ground cumin
3 medium cloves garlic, finely chopped
1 teaspoon salt
1 16-ounce can whole tomatoes
1 6-ounce can tomato paste
1 4-ounce can whole green chiles, seeded and chopped
2 16-ounce cans kidney beans with liquid

1. Melt the lard, butter, or drippings in a large heavy pot over medium heat. Add the onion, celery, and bell pepper and cook until the onion is translucent. Add the sliced mushrooms and cook for an additional five minutes.

2. Combine the meat with the ground chile, oregano, cumin, and garlic. Add this meat-and-spice mixture to the pot. Break up any lumps with a fork and cook, stirring occasionally, until the meat is evenly browned.

3. Stir in the remaining ingredients except the beans. Bring to a boil, then lower the heat and simmer, uncovered, for 1½ hours. Stir occasionally.

4. Add the beans and their liquid and simmer, uncovered, for ½ hour longer. Taste and adjust seasonings.

**Serves: 6**

# Chili à la Franey

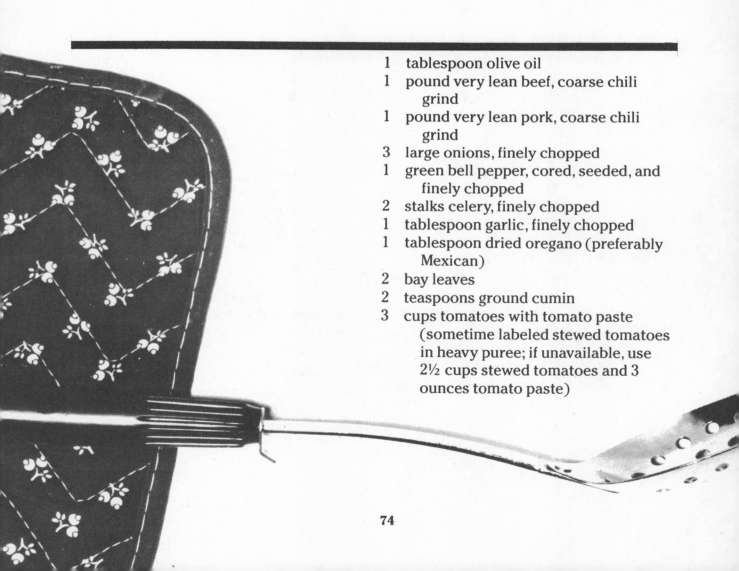

1 tablespoon olive oil
1 pound very lean beef, coarse chili
   grind
1 pound very lean pork, coarse chili
   grind
3 large onions, finely chopped
1 green bell pepper, cored, seeded, and
   finely chopped
2 stalks celery, finely chopped
1 tablespoon garlic, finely chopped
1 tablespoon dried oregano (preferably
   Mexican)
2 bay leaves
2 teaspoons ground cumin
3 cups tomatoes with tomato paste
   (sometime labeled stewed tomatoes
   in heavy puree; if unavailable, use
   2½ cups stewed tomatoes and 3
   ounces tomato paste)

Well-known chef and author Pierre Franey has devised this excellent recipe for chili which can be prepared in practically no time at all.

He suggests garnishing the finished brew with sour cream and lime wedges.

1 cup beef broth
1 cup water
Salt and freshly ground pepper to taste
½ teaspoon chile caribe (see page 26)
2 tablespoons ground red chile (hot, mild, or a combination to taste)
2 cups cooked kidney beans, drained

**1.** If possible, have the beef and pork ground together, or else mix meats together in a bowl.

**2.** Heat the oil in a large heavy pot over medium heat. Add the meat to the pot. Break up any lumps with a fork and cook, stirring occasionally, until the meat is evenly browned.

**3.** Add the onions, green pepper, celery, garlic, oregano, bay leaves, and cumin. Mix well.

**4.** Add the tomatoes, broth, water, salt, pepper, caribe, and ground chile. Bring to a boil, then lower heat and simmer, uncovered, for about 20 minutes. Stir often.

**5.** Add the beans and simmer for 10 minutes longer. Taste and adjust seasonings.

**Serves: 4**

# Hy Abernathy's Georgia Chain-Gang Chili

We can't guarantee that this recipe has prison chain-gang roots but ideally it should be cooked over a two- to three-day period thereby imprisoning you in your kitchen and chaining you to your stove! Seriously, make sure to leave at least four hours of cooking time. If you

1 cup dry Burgundy
½ teaspoon dried thyme
2 bay leaves
4 medium cloves garlic, finely chopped
½ teaspoon freshly ground black pepper
3 pounds beef, any cut, coarse chili grind
3 pounds extra lean beef, coarse chili grind
2 large chicken breasts, skinned and boned
   Water
1 to 2 tablespoons salt
2 tablespoons vegetable oil
2 medium onions, coarsely chopped
3 large pork chops, boned (or 1 small pork roast, about 2½ pounds, trimmed of all fat), coarse chili grind
4 to 16 tablespoons ground mild red chile, to taste
1 teaspoon cayenne pepper
1 teaspoon dried oregano, (preferably Mexican)
½ teaspoon ground cumin

   Dash dried rosemary
1½ cups canned Italian-style tomatoes, crushed
1 16-ounce can tomato sauce
1 8-ounce can Mexican hot-style tomato sauce
1 4-ounce can whole mild green chiles, seeded and chopped
1 4-ounce can pickled jalapeño peppers, finely chopped
2 tablespoons liquid hot pepper sauce
1 tablespoon butter
3 fresh whole green chiles, parched, peeled, seeded, and chopped (see page 26)
½ cup fresh mushrooms, chopped
½ cup Sauterne
12 ounces beer

go the three-day route, marinate the beef overnight, then prepare the chili and cook it very slowly for five or six hours the first day. Let it sit overnight, then cook it for three hours on the second day and again on the third. The creator of this recipe, Hy Abernathy, a 1979 World Champion chili cookoff contestant, says, "Chili should be hot, but some carry this to the point of absurdity. I don't think chili should bring tears to your eyes, but it should produce a few beads of sweat on the brow."

1. In a large non-aluminum (preferably glass or glazed cast iron) bowl make a marinade by combining the burgundy, thyme, bay leaves, garlic, and black pepper. Place all the beef in the bowl and mix lightly to coat the meat well. Cover and refrigerate overnight. (If time is short marinate for 2 hours at room temperature.)

2. Place the chicken breasts in a saucepan with enough water to cover. Add 1 teaspoon salt and simmer over low heat for ½ hour. Remove the chicken reserving the liquid. Chop the chicken breasts fine and reserve.

3. Melt the oil in a large heavy pot. Add the onions and cook until they are translucent.

4. Meanwhile, drain the beef, straining and reserving the marinade. Mix the beef and pork together, then combine the meats with the ground chile, cayenne pepper, oregano, cumin, rosemary, and the rest of the salt. Add this meat-and-spice mixture to the pot with the onions. Break up any lumps with a fork and cook, stirring occasionally, until the meat is evenly browned.

5. Add half the marinade, the reserved chicken, tomatoes, both tomato sauces, jalapeños, and 1 tablespoon of liquid hot pepper sauce to the pot.

6. Melt the butter in a heavy skillet over medium heat. Add the fresh chiles, mushrooms, and a small amount of the Sauterne and cook for 3 minutes. Add this to the pot.

7. Bring to a boil and simmer, uncovered, for at least 3 hours. While the chili is cooking, from time to time stir in the remaining marinade, the remaining Sauterne, and beer. If more liquid is needed, stir in the water the chicken was cooked in. Taste and adjust seasonings.

**Serves: 20**

# Wheat and Meat Chili

Having little meat on hand, but lots of wheat, an Ogden, Utah, chili cook "stretched the stew" with wheat and liked it well enough to let us know about it. Try it if you yen for something different. Whole wheat kernels are available in health-food stores.

1    cup whole wheat kernels, soaked overnight in water to cover
¼    pound beef suet, finely chopped, or ¼ cup lard
2    medium onions, coarsely chopped
1½   pounds beef, coarse chili grind
2    tablespoons ground hot red chile
2    tablespoons ground mild red chile
3    medium cloves garlic, crushed
½    teaspoon dried oregano (preferably Mexican)
2    teaspoons ground cumin
1    teaspoon salt
½    teaspoon chile caribe (see page 26)
1    8-ounce can diced green chiles
1    8-ounce can tomato paste
1    32-ounce can tomato juice

**1.** In a heavy saucepan, boil the presoaked wheat, covered, for 1 hour in the water used for soaking. Add more water as the kernels cook, if necessary.

**2.** Melt the suet or lard in a large heavy pot over medium-high heat. Remove the rendered suet pieces, add the onions to the pot, and cook until they are translucent.

**3.** Combine the beef with the ground chile, garlic, oregano, cumin, and salt to taste. Add this beef-and-spice mixture to the pot with the onions. Break up any lumps with a fork and cook, stirring occasionally, until the meat is evenly browned. Stir in the caribe, green chiles, tomato paste, and tomato juice.

**4.** Drain the wheat, reserving the liquid, and stir in the kernels. Bring to a boil, then lower the heat and simmer uncovered, for 1 hour. If the chili begins to get too dry, add some of the liquid the wheat was cooked in. Taste and adjust seasonings.

**Serves: 4**

78

# Serendipity's Southern Chili

Eastern chili lovers flock to the Serendipity General Store and Restaurant in New York City for this spicy chili. You can make it, or visit Serendipity when you're in the Big Apple.

| | |
|---|---|
| 4 | tablespoons butter |
| 1 | large onion, coarsely chopped |
| 3 | to 4 pounds lean beef, hamburger grind |
| 8 | tablespoons ground hot red chile |
| 4 | tablespoons ground mild red chile |
| 3 | tablespoons ground cumin |
| 3 | medium cloves garlic, crushed |
| 1 | tablespoon freshly ground black pepper |
| 1 | tablespoon salt |
| 1 | tablespoon sugar |
| 1 | 12-ounce can peeled whole tomatoes |
| 4 | 16-ounce cans kidney beans, with liquid |

**1.** Melt the butter in a large heavy pot over medium heat. Add the onion and cook until it is translucent.

**2.** Combine the meat with the ground chile, cumin, garlic, and pepper. Add this meat-and-spice mixture to the pot. Break up any lumps with a fork and cook, stirring occasionally, until the meat is evenly browned.

**3.** Stir in the remaining ingredients. Bring to a boil, then lower the heat and simmer, uncovered, for at least 4 hours but as many as 8 if possible. Stir occasionally. Taste and adjust seasonings.

**Serves: 6 to 8**

# Vegetarian Chili

2½ cups dried kidney beans, soaked
   overnight in water to cover
3 teaspoons salt
1 cup tomato juice
1 cup raw bulghur (cracked wheat —
   available in some supermarkets
   and most health food stores)
2 tablespoons olive oil
2 medium onions, coarsely chopped
4 medium cloves garlic, crushed
3 stalks celery, coarsely chopped
3 carrots, coarsely chopped
3 or 4 tomatoes, peeled, seeded, and
   coarsely chopped
1 tablespoon fresh lemon juice
2 tablespoons ground hot red chile
3 tablespoons ground mild red chile

1 teaspoon ground cumin
½ teaspoon dried oregano
   (preferably Mexican)
1 teaspoon dried basil
   Freshly ground black pepper to
   taste
1½ green bell peppers, cored, seeded,
   and coarsely chopped

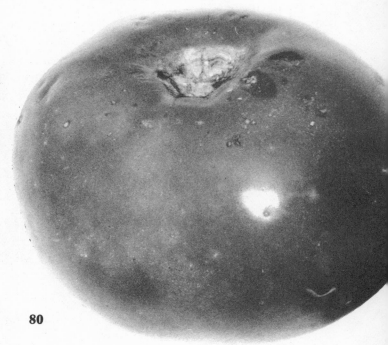

What to do when vegetarian friends or relatives are coming to dinner? Good news—they need not go chili-less. This recipe provides the good taste of chili plus the benefit of complete protein derived from the beans and the bulghur. Serve this brew topped with grated cheese for additional protein and flavor.

**1.** Transfer the kidney beans and the water in which they soaked to a large heavy saucepan. Add 1 teaspoon of the salt and bring to a boil over high heat. Lower the heat and continue boiling the beans, partially covered, until tender, about 1 hour. Watch the water level and add more, if necessary, to keep the beans from scorching.

**2.** Meanwhile, place the tomato juice in another saucepan and bring to a boil over medium heat. Remove from the heat immediately and add the bulghur to the juice. Cover and let stand for 15 minutes. It should be slightly crunchy. Set aside.

**3.** Heat the olive oil in a large heavy pot over medium heat. Add the onions and garlic and cook until the onions are translucent. Add the celery, carrots, tomatoes, lemon juice, and all the spices—including the remaining salt—to the onions and cook, covered, until the vegetables are nearly tender, about 10 to 15 minutes. Add the bell peppers and continue cooking another 10 minutes.

**4.** Add the kidney beans, the water in which they cooked, and the bulghur to the vegetables in the large pot. Stir the mixture thoroughly and simmer for 30 minutes over low heat. The chili may be thick—add water as necessary and stir occasionally making sure the bulghur does not stick to the bottom of the pot. Taste and adjust seasoning.

**Serves: 6 to 8**

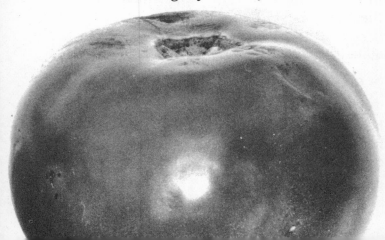

# Authentic Texas Border Chili

**The creator of this gastronomic epic hails from Brownsville, Texas, and insists that you follow his recipe to the letter!**

3 medium tomatoes, peeled, cored, and seeded

1 large Bermuda onion, finely chopped

¼ teaspoon dried oregano (preferably Mexican)

2 teaspoons paprika

5 large cloves garlic, finely chopped

4 pounds beef shank, coarse chili grind

1 tablespoon lard, butter, or bacon drippings

4 bunches (about 24) scallions, cleaned and chopped

5 green bell peppers, cored, seeded and coarsely chopped

5 fresh or canned, pickled serrano chiles, seeded and finely chopped (for fresh, see page 26)

1 pound chorizo sausage or other spicy hot sausage (not Italian), sliced

4 medium cloves garlic, finely chopped

2 teaspoons salt

4 tablespoons ground hot red chile

4 tablespoons ground mild red chile

3 tablespoons prepared cumin seeds*
Water or beer

**1.** Puree the first four ingredients plus one clove of the garlic in a blender or food processor (using the steel blade). Scrape the mixture into a large heavy pot and add the beef.

**2.** Melt the lard, butter, or bacon drippings in a heavy skillet over medium heat. Add the scallions, bell peppers, serrano chiles, chorizo, and the remaining garlic, and cook until the onions are translucent and the chorizo is browned.

**3.** Stir the vegetables into the beef-and-tomato mixture. Add the salt, ground chile, cumin, and enough water or beer to cover. Bring to a boil over medium-high heat, then lower the heat and simmer, uncovered, for 4 to 6 hours. Taste and adjust seasonings.

**Serves: 10 to 12**

*To prepare the cumin seeds, place them in a 300°F. oven for a few minutes until lightly browned. Remove seeds from the oven and crush them with a mallet.

# Clyde's Chili

Easternized and somewhat "conveniencized," Clyde's — a Washington, D.C. restaurant — chili is a favorite of the capital set. I've cut this quick cooking recipe down from it's gargantuan, restaurant proportions, but kept its irresistible taste.

3   tablespoons cooking oil
2   large onions, coarsely chopped
3   pounds beef, coarse chili grind
2   tablespoons Worcestershire sauce
3   medium cloves garlic, finely chopped
4   tablespoons ground hot chile
4   tablespoons ground mild red chile
2   teaspoons ground cumin
1   teaspoon dried oregano (preferably
      Mexican)
2   teaspoons salt
1   16-ounce can kidney beans in chili
      sauce
15  ounces chili sauce (ketchup type)

**1.** Heat the oil in a Dutch oven or heavy 5-quart saucepan over medium heat. Add the onions and cook until they are translucent.

**2.** Add the beef to the pot with the onions. Break up any lumps with a fork and cook, stirring occasionally, until the meat is evenly browned. Add the Worcestershire sauce and garlic and cook for 3 minutes.

**3.** Stir in the ground chile, cumin, oregano, and salt and cook, uncovered, for 5 minutes.

**4.** Add the beans and chili sauce and simmer, uncovered, for 1 hour. Taste and adjust seasonings.

**Serves: 6 to 8**

# Bert Greene's Peppered Chili

7 tablespoons butter
2 medium cloves garlic, finely chopped
4 onions, finely chopped
1 large green bell pepper, cored, seeded, and finely chopped
1¼ pounds beef round, hamburger grind
1 tablespoon vegetable oil
1½ pounds beef shoulder, trimmed and cut into strips 2 inches long and ½ inch wide
3 tablespoons ground mild red chile
3 large tomatoes, peeled, cored, and chopped
1 teaspoon sugar
1 bay leaf, crumbled
4 fresh basil leaves, chopped, or a pinch dried basil
Pinch dried thyme
½ teaspoon paprika
½ teaspoon cayenne pepper

½ teaspoon ground allspice
1 dried whole red chile pepper, crushed, or 2 tablespoons chile caribe (see page 26)
1 teaspoon soy sauce
½ teaspoon liquid hot pepper sauce
6 fresh or canned, pickled serrano chiles, finely chopped (for fresh, see page 26)
½ cup dry red wine
¾ cup beef broth
1 teaspoon salt
½ teaspoon freshly ground black pepper
3 cups cooked kidney beans, drained

84

Bert Greene, a popular food writer, contributed this recipe which originally appeared in his book *Kitchen Bouquets*. He thinks this oven-made recipe is the best of his chili collection. Serve it over rice to strong friends—and proceed with some caution with the serrano chiles.

**1.** Melt 3 tablespoons of the butter in a large heavy skillet over medium heat. Add half the garlic, half the onions, and all the green pepper and cook for 5 minutes.

**2.** Make a large well in the center of the vegetables and place the ground beef in the center. Raise the heat and cook, stirring and scraping the skillet with a metal spatula. Gradually stir in the surrounding vegetables and cook until the meat is evenly browned. Transfer this mixture to a Dutch oven.

**3.** Heat the vegetable oil and 1 tablespoon of the butter in the skillet. Sauté the beef shoulder, a few strips at a time, over high heat until it is well browned. Transfer the strips to a plate as they are done. Lower the heat, then wipe out the skillet with paper toweling. Return beef strips to the skillet. Stir in the ground chile and cook 3 minutes over low heat. Transfer to the Dutch oven.

**4.** Melt the remaining butter in the skillet over medium heat. Add the remaining onions and garlic and cook for 3 minutes. Stir in the tomatoes, sugar, and bay leaf and cook for 10 minutes. Transfer the mixture to the Dutch oven.

**5.** Stir all the remaining ingredients except the beans into the Dutch oven. Bake, covered, in a 300°F. oven for 3 hours.

**6.** Stir in the beans; bake ½ hour longer.

**Serves: 4 to 6**

85

# Australian Dinkum Chili

½ pound package bacon
2 tablespoons vegetable oil
2 medium onions, coarsely chopped
1 stalk celery, coarsely chopped
1 green bell pepper, cored, seeded and
   coarsely chopped
2 pounds top beef sirloin, cut into 1-inch
   cubes
1 pound beef, hamburger grind
1 pound pork, hamburger grind
4 tablespoons ground hot red chile
3 tablespoons ground mild red chile
2 medium cloves garlic, finely chopped
1 tablespoon dried oregano (preferably
   Mexican)
1 teaspoon ground cumin
2 12-ounce cans beer (preferably
   Australian)
1 14½-ounce can whole tomatoes
   Boomerang (optional but authentic)
3 teaspoons brown sugar

**1.** Fry the bacon in a skillet over medium heat. Drain the strips on paper toweling and cut into ½-inch dice and reserve.

**2.** Heat the oil in a large heavy pot over medium heat. Add the onions, celery, and green pepper and cook until the onions are translucent.

**3.** Combine all the beef and pork with the ground chile, garlic, oregano, and cumin. Add this meat-and-spice mixture to the pot. Break up any lumps with a fork and cook, stirring occasionally, until the meat is evenly browned.

Chili madness has affected another country with a cowboy culture . . . our friends "down under" have the same passion for chili as we Yanks. Why, they even have a National Chili Archives in Tibooburra, New South Wales and an entire cult of chili eaters on the auto-racing circuit. This recipe for Dinkum Chili ("dinkum" is the Australian slang for "authentic") has won the Annual Western Australian Winter Championship Chili Cookoff at Kunanaggi Well. It was created by Australia's racing team. This version has been adapted for American ingredients.

**4.** Add the beer, tomatoes, and reserved bacon to the pot. Bring to a boil, then lower the heat and simmer, uncovered, for 1½ hours. Wave a boomerang over the pot 14 times each hour from this point on. (This is definitely optional adding no noticeable flavor, just a touch of authenticity and humor.) Stir for 3 minutes. Taste, adjust seasonings, and add more beer if desired. Simmer for 2½ hours longer.

**5.** Add the brown sugar and simmer for 15 minutes longer, vigorously waving the boomerang over the pot.

**Serves: 8**

Here's a list of authentic chili ingredients the likes of which you've probably never seen before. They are listed as they appear in the original recipe for Dinkum Chili.

| | |
|---|---|
| 500 | grams Wallaroo bacon |
| 2 | tablespoons vegetable oil |
| 1 | medium brown onion, chopped |
| 1 | white onion, chopped |
| 2 | stalks celery, chopped |
| 1 | green pepper, diced |
| 1 | kilogram coarsely chopped red kangaroo shank |
| 500 | grams coarsely chopped gray kangaroo steak |
| 500 | grams ground emu ham |
| 2 | cloves garlic |
| 31½ | grams Tasmanian light red chile |
| 31½ | grams Wooroorooka chile |
| 26½ | grams Mount Isa dark red chile |
| 140 | grams oregano |
| 1 | fluid gram cumin |
| 1 | 740m/l bottle Australian beer |
| 1 | 4ll can whole tomatoes |
| | Boomerang |
| 3 | fluid drams brown sugar |

# A Red Chili Nightmare

| | |
|---|---|
| 1 cup dried pinto beans | 12 whole dried red chiles, crushed then soaked to soften in hot water to cover, and drained (or 1½ cups chile caribe, see page 26) |
| 4 to 5 cups water | |
| 2 tablespoons lard | |
| 1 tablespoon bacon drippings | |
| 1 medium onion, coarsely chopped | |
| 12 ounces hot country-style pork sausage | 1½ ounces milk chocolate, broken into small pieces |
| 1 pound lean beef, coarse chili grind | 1 6-ounce can tomato paste |
| 4 cloves garlic, crushed | 2 tablespoons vinegar |
| 1 teaspoon anise | 3 teaspoons lemon juice |
| ½ teaspoon coriander seeds, crushed | 1 soft tortilla, chopped |
| ½ teaspoon fennel seeds | Salt |
| ½ teaspoon ground cloves | |
| 1 1-inch stick cinnamon, ground | |
| 1 teaspoon freshly ground black pepper | |
| 1 teaspoon paprika | |
| 1 whole nutmeg, ground | |
| 1 teaspoon ground cumin | |
| 2 teaspoons dried oregano (preferably Mexican) | |
| 4 tablespoons sesame seeds | |
| 1 cup almonds, blanched, skins removed, and crushed fine | |

If you're an adventurous cook and you want a batch of chili that will fill the house with fragrant wonderfulness, this gourmet delight is for you—despite the name. The pinto beans must be soaked overnight before you begin.

**1.** Place the rinsed beans in a bowl, add 2 to 3 cups of water and soak overnight. Check the beans occasionally and add water as necessary to keep them moist.

**2.** Pour the beans and the water in which they were soaked into a heavy saucepan and add 2 to 3 more cups of water. Bring to a boil over medium-high heat, then lower heat and simmer, partially covered, for about 45 minutes, until the beans are cooked but still firm. Check occasionally and add water if necessary. Drain the beans, reserving the cooking liquid.

**3.** Melt the lard in a heavy skillet over medium heat. Add the beans and lightly fry them in the lard.                    Set aside.

**4.** Melt the drippings in a large heavy pot over medium heat. Add the onion and cook until it is translucent.

**5.** Combine the sausage and the beef with all the spices up through the oregano. Add this meat-and-spice mixture to the pot with the onion. Break up any lumps with a fork and cook, stirring occasionally, until the meat is very well browned.

**6.** Add the reserved bean-cooking liquid to the pot. Stir in all the remaining ingredients. Bring to a boil, then lower the heat and cook, uncovered, for ½ hour. Add the beans and simmer, uncovered, for ½ hour longer. Stir occasionally. Add water only if necessary to maintain the consistency of a chunky soup.

**7.** Taste when curiosity becomes unbearable and courage is strong. Adjust seasonings.

**Serves: 4**

# Mail Order Sources

It is a good idea to write for a catalog and price list to see what these sources have available before you order.

**Arizona**
El Molina
117 S. 22nd Street
Phoenix, Ariz. 85034

Sasabe Store
P.O. Box 7
Sasabe, Ariz. 85704

**California**
La Palma
2884 24th Street
San Francisco, Calif. 94110

**Illinois**
Casa Esteiro
2719 W. Division
Chicago, Ill. 60622

**New York**
Casa Moneo
210 W. 14th Street
New York, N.Y. 10011

Pecos River Spice Company
P.O. Box 680
New York, N.Y. 10021

H. Roth and Son
1577 First Avenue
New York, N.Y. 10021

**Texas**
Ashley's Inc.
6590 Montana Avenue
El Paso, Tex. 79925

Simon David Grocery Store
711 Inwood Road
Dallas, Tex. 78207

Frank Pizzini
202 Produce Row
San Antonio, Tex. 78207

**Washington, D.C.**
Casa Pena
1636 17th Street N.W.
Washington, D.C. 20009

# Index